How to Write a Bench

Poetry and Art

David Hummon

Finishing Line Press
Georgetown, Kentucky

How to Write a Bench

Copyright © 2026 by David Hummon
ISBN 979-8-89990-309-0 First Edition
All rights reserved under International and Pan-American Copyright Conventions. No part of this book may be reproduced in any manner whatsoever without written permission from the publisher, except in the case of brief quotations embodied in critical articles and reviews.

Publisher: Leah Huete de Maines
Editor: Christen Kincaid
Cover Art: *Bench*, watercolor and ink, Chesnut Park, Palm Harbor, Florida, David Hummon
Author Photo: Mary Hummon
Cover Design: David Hummon

Order online: www.finishinglinepress.com
also available on amazon.com

Author inquiries and mail orders:
Finishing Line Press
PO Box 1626
Georgetown, Kentucky 40324
USA

Contents

~1~

How to Write a Bench 1
At the Arboretum 3
At Seventy-Five
    Birthday 5
    Attached 6
    Road Map 7
    The Chorus 8
    Writing 9
    Frames 10
A True Account of Talking to My Suitcase in the Basement 11

~2~

Family Reunion, 1895 15
Homemade, 1939 16
Dear Mom and Dad 17
Day Three, 1946 19
Oral History 20
The Hall 22
Drawing Dad 23
The Meeting 24
Seed Time, Vermont 25
In the Northeast Kingdom 26
She Asked Me 27
Learning to Walk 28
At the Local Garage 29
Whose Woods 31
What Wants Doing 32
Generations 33

~3~

There Was an Old Woman 37
The Cane 38
Doppelganger 39
Anxiety 40

Good Friday 41
My Rollator 42
Appendectomy 43
How to Self-Isolate 44
Confession 46

~4~

On Looking at my Painting of Sunflowers 49
Ode to my Sketchbook 51
Bloom 53
Works on Paper 54
Landscape Workshop 55
Dorothea Lange: A Gallery
    Imperial Valley, California 56
    High Plains 57
    Composed 58
    Soup Kitchen 59
Sisters 60
Likeness 61
Searching for Fitz 62
Lines 67

~5~

Florida 71
Hats—A Love Song 73
The Goddess of Fun 74
The Truth about Sourdough 75
French Fries 76
Ritual Food 77
Threshold 78
Paddle 79
Invocation 81
Some Mornings Everything is a Poem 82
Arlington Matins 83

Acknowledgments 84
A Note on Ekphrastic Poems 85
A Note on the Author 87

For Mary

~ 1 ~

Glory Be to Trees, The Arnold Arboretum,
Boston, ink and watercolor

HOW TO WRITE A BENCH

>*Just peel back the folds over your heart*
>*and shine into it*
>*the strongest light that streams*
>*from your eyes, or somewhere else.*
>   Laura Hershey, "How to Write a Poem"

Really? Maybe, one way for sure, but hardly for me.
I've spent years creating those folds, and I little need
more heartache, metaphoric or not, more anguish,
more Glück.
                    I'd rather write a bench instead,
prosaic for sure, but better than hearts, confession,
the fire of passion, cutting, death. What I need today
when my legs are tired.
                    A basic bench will do,
will more than do, preferably in the shade, well-placed,
a civilized gesture, like in Paris, Central Park, or the cluster
behind the library for reading. No wonder
people use benches for elegies:

. . Love, Duty and Character Personified . . .
. . . bridge, friend, mentor to youth . . . In Memoriam / William J
and Dorothy Day /"There will stars over the place forever."

Benches come with a point of view, out: to the pond,
the gravestones, or the CVS where middle schoolers
with their phones hang out, flirt.
                      Best, they come
with a companion. There's room for two voices, someone
to speak, someone to listen, not like a chair:
the love you brought with you, the dogwalker,
the ghosts who join you in silence.

Benches tend to be well-built, strong, horizontal,
like a line of poetry, except for curving arms to hold you,
to lend a hand getting up and down—
the best are even beautiful.
                      Please sit a bit,
while I cross out the first stanza, or maybe not.

We can thank the worn wood, the sturdy legs,
those who have been here before, and will come after
to rest, to watch, to talk, maybe to draw
or even write a poem.

AT THE ARBORETUM

> *What is all this juice and all this joy?*
> Gerard Manley Hopkins, "Spring"

Glory be to trees,
to grace-filled symmetry
halo-crowned, radiant
with green-gold leaves.

> To garden kneelers, makers,
> groundkeepers, pruners
> and righteous rakers.

Glory be to catkins,
to caterpillar flowers,
dangly, twisty, festooning
birch bark branches.

> To preschoolers, harnessed
> in line, their centipede feet
> crawling lawns, with teacher-head
> and tail.

Glory be to lilacs, lavender,
purple-violet, white, unruly,
scenting memories of childhood
bouquets and clapboard houses.

> To lilac pilgrims, festive,
> clustered flower friends,
> snapping photos, mementoes
> diligent, devout.

Glory be to greening grass
snowed apple-petal white,
to dandelion ghosts tossing seeds
in windborne flight.

To all bench sitters, resting, retired,
binoculared birders, twiggy joggers,
dogwalkers, however groomed,
that disheveled barefoot man . . .

And even me, bobbing, lifted,
toe-walking, morning-bloomed.

AT SEVENTY-FIVE

BIRTHDAY

It's hard to ignore turning 75.
Thirty was easy (I don't even recall that turn),
forty flashed by in the rear-view mirror,
but three-quarters of a century sounds different—
that's historical time, not biography, not even generations.

The only thing close was sixteen,
I do remember that: the learner's permit,
the driver's test, picking up my girlfriend
to go to a movie, no parents, parking
down the block. That was a date.

Seventy-five takes the blinders off:
people don't offer you a seat for nothing,
all those old folks at the symphony are you,
and there's the detritus of walkers in the garage,
your suitcase, packed with medical stuff, not clothes.

And yet living history is good, too:
you do learn from mistakes, sometimes,
patience is easier, and you know that each life
contains several lives. Your next one starts today,
though you can't really be sure, at seventy-five.

ATTACHED

At seventy-five, I feel closer to my dog.
He barks at delivery men, grinning at their retreat.
He doesn't complain when ill; just withdraws and naps.
He doesn't understand so much and doesn't understand he doesn't.
He does understand smells and urine, treats on top of kibble,
        lying on his back for a belly rub.
He's terribly attached to my wife, and me, too, for that matter.
He's ready to go anytime, which reminds me to go, to the park.
He likes to sit on me, climbing on my chest like Whitman's
        tongue-licking soul, only to fall asleep.

ROAD MAP

At seventy-five, this neglected city street
underfoot looks like a map of the United States
drawn by a fourth grader, state lines etched
in asphalt from excavations
of gas lines, sewers, water mains
and other arterial repairs.

Some slender horizontal patches stretch
to the curb like Kentucky and Tennessee,
others extend up-down like Vermont
and New Hampshire. Large rectangles
and squares—Wyoming, Colorado, Nebraska—
abut with off-set corners

while dogleg California veers to nowhere.
Potholes parody the Great Lakes
with their uneven shorelines; fine cracks
connect, growing wider and wider
like the Mississippi, Missouri, and Ohio,
coursing downhill across the continent.

A decent map, this geography of childhood,
where I once memorized capitals and colored
the states with crayons of ignorance and hope,
though today I have misplaced Topeka,
which could be worse, compared to other readings
of this worn road and my life at seventy-five.

THE CHORUS

> *All God's creatures got a place in the choir*
> *Some sing low and some sing higher.*
> Bill Staines, 1947 - 2021

When I hear "Hark the Herald" on the radio my mind sings tenor
with eighteen-year-old abandon, prancing around the sopranos
with notes light as reindeer hooves, clapping unison hands
for the insistent "Joyful, all ye nations," before resolving with a grin
to the sweet third of "newborn King."

It's good, fits the holiday spirit when I too was new born
and knew that male angels, if there were any, were certainly tenors,
though I kid myself here, conveniently forgetting infant howls
and a boy soprano lost to coming of age
and sweet denial.

When I actually sing with the herald angels, hymnal in hand,
on Christmas eve, I flit between melody and bass
like a rowdy angel, finding solace in the tonic foundation
of the lower clef, companionship with the ox and ass on melody,
and joy incarnate, not having arrived late with the other wise men
at seventy-five.

WRITING

At seventy-five, lines run short,
tetrameter is typical
sometimes a beat more, sometimes less.
Blank verse is difficult to write.

Is it simply my age—like climbing
a hill, I run out of breath,
or forget where I am going?
Once around the block is enough.

Or could it be our age,
where people write with their thumbs,
measure text in characters,
tell lies that take your breath away?

Still, I work to find proper length,
Stretching out lines for contradiction,
for ambiguity, zig-zagging this way, that, and both.
Worshiping more than one god often takes long lines

and I remember short is good too,
like an afternoon nap, her touch,
this moment,
this breath.

FRAMES

> *and the poets are at their windows*
> *because it is their job for which*
> *they are paid nothing every Friday afternoon.*
>   Billy Collins, "Monday"

At seventy-five, I'm done with this age
in two months. Not sure where it went,
maybe flew to Florida, no serious time
down there—spring in February—but
it no longer frames everything
like *not-getting-enough-done*
or *it-doesn't-matter-anyway*.

There's the old cliché, too—
how time speeds up as you get older:
remember waiting for your eighth birthday?
Or maybe worse: two months is a year now,
like dog-years.

Seventy-five still pokes me occasionally.
That pain in the knee, newspaper obituaries,
and she said at the workshop, "Oh, you're old,"
to the guy who said he was 42,
and I rocketed to *The Meaning of Life,*
The Universe, and Everything,
too big a frame, like goal posts at each end
of the field waving their arms in the air,
but better than *seventy-five*, too small
a field of play. Better just roam here
on La Grande Jatte with the monkey
in Sunday afternoon presence
and forget about the painted frame.

But it's so hard, you can't live
without them unless you're Buddha,
and window frames are useful
for seeing out and letting in light—
Collins got that right.

A TRUE ACCOUNT OF TALKING TO MY SUITCASE IN THE BASEMENT

"About time you got me down
and opened me up. I'm suffocating:
haven't been out for fresh air and sun
since we moved here. Have you no shame?"

"Sorry, I didn't think it mattered," I said,
pulling the cardboard suitcase off the shelf,
unsnapping the tarnished brass clasps.
"You've been dry and safe."

"There are more important things than safe.
What brings you rummaging today? Photos,
love letters, that juvenilia?"

                "Poems, mostly—just curious."
"I can save you time on that: they're terrible,
sophomoric, filled with thee's-and-thou's,
dying leaves and gothic nights, golden moons,
Greek-goddesses. God, it's embarrassing.
Lived with them for sixty years. I know."

                "I was in high school."
"What are you hoping to find? Intimations
of greatness, reasons for regret, springlets
of the soul? Forget it. Your photos were better:
you looked and composed. The girlfriend
poems are okay—'messed her hair'—
you liked her, and I can imagine the rest."

                    "I was in high . . ."
"You already said that. What's your excuse now?
Why aren't you writing new stuff, not excavating?"

        "I am. Can't do it all the time. And it's hard."
"Okay, a break then: let's go to the beach—
dump this stuff, get your swim trunks, pencils, paper,
corn chips—anyplace out of here.
You pick, I'll navigate."

                                            "Now?"
"What's the problem? Afraid of sunburn?
Having fun? Being seen with me?
No wheels, I admit, but I work, sort of.
You drive and I'll read your new stuff.
Can't be any worse than this basement.
If it rains, we can read O'Hara on the porch.
He was a beach guy and liked cities
and art like you."

                        "Well…"
"You still don't get it, do you? I have a handle,
that's for your right hand, the one you write with.
Pick me up, and let's go. Even lunch would be good,
you could write a poem about a hamburger and a Coke."

~ 2 ~

Homemade, sepia ink with sepia watercolor

FAMILY REUNION, 1895

So many ancestors, one hundred forty-two,
posed for the picture at the county fairground
on the wooden benches of the grandstand,
stacked like mason jars with lids and seals
on shelves in grandmother's pantry.

Eight little ones on laps, just jelly jars,
some bonneted, some capped;
bouquets of girls, hair center-parted,
some with long braids or draping curls;
their mothers, hair carefully arranged
gathered, pulled up or back, orderly,
mirroring the matriarchs, Mary, Amanda,
Alma, Eliza, Sarah, bunned, pinned, upright
like their backs, some topped with black hats,
flowered, feathered, eminently respectable.

Tufts of boys, brothers baled together,
brown hair, tousled mops or side-parted;
young men clustered on the high benches,
clean shaven, hair combed and parted;
farm fathers next to their wives, white foreheads
with weathered cheeks and chins, good crops of hair,
the townsmen, barber-shop trim, spotless,
mustached, with ties; the patriarchs,
Peter, John, Levi, David, Simon,
full beards and hidden mouths, white-grey,
ample shocks of hair, except one, to the side,
with a thinning top, dark heavy eyelashes
who could have been my brother.

Exhibited on the wall at my folks' house,
a photo of a photo, enlarged, reproduced
like generations—none of whom look like me—
small-town, rural families, gathered to celebrate
shared understanding, a harvest of proper hair,
exposed ears, and a place in the grandstand.

HOMEMADE, 1939

for Aunt Jan, ninety-seven

Midwestern, true, and from the thirties,
even a grown daughter and her father
with wire-rimmed glasses and bib overalls—
but this photograph is no *American Gothic*.

No tight dour faces, framed in carpenter gothic,
no vertical board-and-batten siding, arched
gable window, no backdrop of perfect trees
from the woodland of sacred shapes.

Just a black and white snapshot with border,
brother and sister close but not touching,
their father, a body's width to the right,
standing in front of overgrown apple trees,

real trees, real men, farmers, at home in their bodies,
sleeves rolled up for the heat of the day. Center stage
this eighteen-year-old poses in her taffeta black gown—
lace inset on the bodice, rhinestone spaghetti straps,

not for church, not for the farm, not for the town—
and smiles, pleased, 4-H proud, modeling her dress,
her hair, her dream, gazing out to somewhere,
singing and dancing all the way to New York,

the same year Judy sang *Over the Rainbow*.

DEAR DAD AND MOM

> *for my father, who wrote five letters to his parents*
> *in these words in the months before and after his 97th birthday.*

Surprised to get a letter from Serge?
Well, I still can write and I think of you two every day.

How is farming going? I miss climbing on the Allis Chalmers
 or the John Deere. Brother Norm was always more at home
with the horses than I was, and you, too, Dad.

I wish we could talk politics and farming.
We used to have good bull sessions.
So many people are so conservative
they find it hard to entertain a new idea.

I'm wondering if you can keep warm in your house.
I forget what you heat by besides the kitchen stove.

You were wise parents, strict and generous. As I look back,
I am grateful you stepped in when I was foolish.
That's what a child needs. Yet a young person needs to be encouraged,
and you got that, too.
So I did well in school.

Some children inherit parents who don't pass on values
that give their kids a good start. We can thank God
human beings turn out as well as they do!

I hope your health is holding.
I think of you every day in some way or other.
Your five kids need your support.

The larger event in my life is the loss of Doris.
We were together for 69 years, an Ohio farm boy
and a Kansas Methodist minister's daughter.

We only produced two boys, but they were guys
we were proud of. We wanted a girl
but that never happened.

I am happy these days. I'm glad I chose the ministry.
And the girl from Kansas to join me. She was one
to keep her spirits up. And to look at both sides
of a problem. I hope to see her in heaven!
and you people too!

I'm in a good place.
Dave, my son, looks in on me almost daily.
Losing Pat has been a real blow for Dave.
I could give up Doris in my 90's but
Dave is in his 60s and faces life alone.
I support him as best I can.

I'll be 97 this June the 27th. I'm living in Massachusetts,
a widower after losing Doris from Kansas.
Life takes strange turns but it has been good through it all.

This is a special month in that I'll be 97 this year, 2014.
Figures don't fool us. But we suddenly feel old.
I've had a good life.

I've been meaning to write you, but I don't seem to get it done.
It's not that I'm so terribly busy. It's just I don't sit down and do it.
Age is beginning to tell I guess.
June went by the other day and my 97th birthday.
That shouldn't be an excuse, but I guess it partly is.
And almost every day I catch myself thinking,
"I wonder what they're doing down on the farm."

So my love to you each day. Sincerely, Serge
I'll continue to be in touch. Your son, Serge
Your son Serge who gives thanks for you two!
I'll stop here for now, Your son, Serge

DAY THREE

Before I was me,
with the softest hair
lumpy head and scabbed nose

before anyone thought
of haircuts or blue
or baby powder

she held me
and called me *David*
unexpectedly

and dad gathered lights,
his camera, and took
a photo of his beloved

recovered, her hair
washed, combed, arranged
holding me outward

to the world
light glinting in my eyes
and made me official.

        after a family photograph,
        Rapid River, Michigan, 1946

ORAL HISTORY

I don't remember talking with my dad as a child
although I'm sure I did.

He taught me how to wash the Chevy on Saturday morning,
how to drive a nail and countersink a screw,
how to paddle properly: the J-stroke to go straight when alone,
later how to work the darkroom: read a negative, crop,
run a test strip, expose, bring up an image,

important things in and of themselves
coupling words and deeds, moral matters
freighted with lessons of work and play,
doing things right, learning to see in the dark.
But he had his life, his work, his travel, and mom,
and I had mine: Lowell School, the lake and swimming,
my bike, Char, Kent, playing *Clue,* making models
and blowing them up, doing nothing,
and the blessings of boredom.

By high school, I noticed he talked to everyone,
true democrat that he was, which could be annoying,
everyone was interesting, mattered, had something to say,
though he never said that

and education was the key, though he never said that either,
the proverbial road, it was just there, of course,
learn, study the text, sometimes question, turn the page
on your dad and mom, your girlfriend, your faith,
though by then that was a soliloquy at best,

maybe you'll find your way, even come back,
maybe not, but tell your own story.

In his nineties we talked, son and dad,
the call and response of chit-chat
baseball when he could still follow the game,
ice cream, the weather, and sometimes
not so everyday stuff, Obama and civil rights,
how the big bang didn't really matter,

and toward the end, when work and decades
were lost to memory, he recounted youthful matters,
odes to back then, the depression, Roosevelt and Debs,
his first car, doing chores and Ohio mud, potatoes,
a high school teacher who cared, and Shakespeare,

even Christmas as a child, when he got an orange,
and for special a scooter to share with his brother and sister.

THE HALL

At ninety-one, the hallway impressed him—
floral carpeted floors, the cavalcade of mass-produced oil paintings,
the changing holiday decorations, the light classical music—
half a football field long, and wide, too,
suitable for electric wheelchairs, the ice cream cart,
and us, walking side by side.

"It's a long hall," he often remarked, smiling and proud,
"fancy for a farm boy from Ohio,"
though he worked most of his life
in The Loop and Manhattan.

To visit mom in the nursing home next door,
he took the emergency stairs, steel and concrete,
two flights, thirty-two steps, three times a day, for three years,
rather than walk the hall to the elevator.

"Quicker," he would report, but more to his purpose,
right, straight-forward, unadorned, in line with steadfast love.

Seven years later in a nursing home,
I pushed his wheelchair out of his room,
by the nursing station, down the linoleum corridor,
scrubbed clean, past doors numbered and charted,
to the coffee lounge. On good days, he remarked,
"Long hall," as we arrived and added "yes" to the coffee.

Now, ninety-nine, toppled by a stroke,
he rides slumped over, wordless,
even when we stop for coffee
at the end of the hall.

DRAWING DAD

I drew his face to be with him—at first
a few quick sketches, him in his canvas hat,
him listening to Beethoven, him sipping coffee,
him singing with the hospice worker.

Sometimes I even got a likeness,
the bushy eyebrows, the scales on his pate,
the proportions right and that *yes-that's-him,*
though you can't see inside.

Now I see the changes: his glasses disappeared
with his sight, the sport coats retired to the closet,
and his face thinned out, disclosing the skull
beneath, and I used ink more and more,

as I got stronger, more direct, willing
to etch the surface . . . but mostly him
sleeping, the one time he would hold still
in an unconscious pose.

It became something for me to do, too,
waiting for him to wake, to talk a bit more,
something to do with him, too, when talking
ended, and there was only waiting.

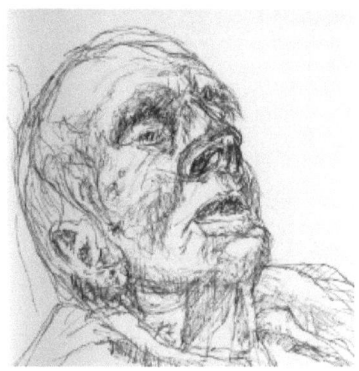

Serge Hummon, December 2016, ink drawing, sketchbook

THE MEETING

Unlikely pair: her hospice nurse, a nun,
to oversee her care. Mom's ninety-one—
Protestant, baptized by her father,
a Kansas pastor; married a minister.
Two years in bed and few complaints—
clean sheets, yes, but what can you expect: the coffee
hot, toast with homemade jam? The lame to walk?
Not her, her faith; so now this time to talk.

"I'm ready," she says " . . . but not today,"
pauses: "but sooner rather than later."
And the nun: "When, we don't decide, He does."
"*She* does," mom amends, trading glances.
"Okay, *She*," the nun replies, "She." Smiling,
they bow, pray—begin this work of dying.

SEED TIME, VERMONT

Mom built the greenhouse off the kitchen,
south facing for light, warmth, a stay against short days,

cold nights—geraniums, begonias, a Norfolk pine
for Christmas lights. And come mud season,

tomatoes, seeds in warming trays for setting out late May;
sweet cherries in a corner tub with poles and strings

for summer clusters, like dangling ornaments,
ripe red, right at hand for salads, handy snacks,

who knows. I used to grow my own in whiskey barrels,
but now I keep window-box geraniums and basil

in clay pots, fresh leaves to pinch and place atop
tomatoes—so pungent, bitter, sweet.

IN THE NORTHEAST KINGDOM

for my mother and father

They gather in the village this grey morn
some, right here, where the school once stood,
children waiting for the morning bell,
scattered across the wet grass
like mottled windfalls from the crabapple tree;
a solider, perched upon a sugar maple stump,
admiring the granite walk he helped to lay
before he marched to the Civil War.

Up Church Street, neighbors I loved as a young man,
Pat, mother of five, the best square dancer in town
who swung me with caring abandon
on Saturday night in the Academy gym,
Howard, ensconced in his Adirondack chair,
white beard flecked with pipe ash, lecturing summer guests
on the exquisite pleasures of fresh-picked August corn.

At the top of the hill at the cemetery gate my folks,
dad, dressed for a sunny July 4th in his Bean shorts
and straw hat, Nikon around his neck, mom in a denim dress
she made, holding his hand, ready for a family portrait.

We walk to see the plot where I will place their ashes,
mom doesn't care but nods approval, dad photographs
the glorious view toward Harvey's Lake,
a postcard he took so many times before he died.

SHE ASKED ME

to trim her hair
in the summer place that August
just days before our wedding.

She wet it, draping a frayed
towel over her leotard top
and stood straight and still.

It was wet-brown, dark as her eyes
and as I combed it out she said,
"Just a little, not too much."

She wore her hair up
at the wedding—a lace ribbon
around her neck

to match her old fashioned dress,
lace white with puffy sleeves
and a hem that brushed the grass—

until the cake was cut
and she kicked off her sandals
and pulled her hair down

around her face and it curved
as it fell, matching the smile
she gave me.

LEARNING TO WALK

for Pat, 1945 -2014

I don't remember learning to walk the first time.
I assume I first toddled, handhold to handhold,
rising, walking, falling, and rising again.
Then later, with greater skill, rose unaided,
bent at the waist, knees locked,
bottom pointed to the sky,
unfolding upward like a jack knife,
ready to carve the world with steady steps.

I recall fragments of the second:
my fourteenth year flat in bed
cast-bound from chest to toe,
strapped like Frankenstein's monster
on a titling table to test if would faint upright;
standing, crutches gripped, weight on my hands,
swinging my body through,
propping open doors with a single crutch,
conquering the fear of stairs.

In grief, I live the third:
though I am stable, the world rises
and falls when I venture out,
I open doors, they close unbidden, cutting time
in pieces, before and after, then and now,
I cope with stairs, but courage fails on level ground.
I toddle, relearning to swing
my body through each day
and walk without a hand to hold.

AT THE LOCAL GARAGE

Outrageous Dependability Starts Here.
Interstate Batteries

The room doubles as an office and place to wait,
two metal desks tucked in toward the back,
one with a roller chair and old beige computer;
the other with a printer, neatly stacked receipts,
and small boxes of parts with taped invoices,
like orders at the take-out. Above the desks,
shelves: on the lowest, a faded photograph
of a middle-aged couple, plastic model cars
from the 1950s, a wooden tow truck for kids,
a mockup of a V-8 engine. Up top, *Quaker State,*
Valvoline, Thrust Starting Fluid, Dry Gas.

Morning light from the large south-facing window
warms the room; scraggly dry geraniums grace
the windowsill. "Looking forward to better weather, Beth?"
Mark appears from the garage to get her keys.
"Isn't everyone?" Beth makes her way to a chair
by the red iron gumball machine, removing a worn
Don't Cry Big Bird from the seat. "Oil's down
so cheap now, I've been using more." "I use wood,"
Mark says, "but burned more oil when I had pneumonia."

For twenty-four years I've waited here,
for our first family car, the white Century,
her green Villager, my commuter Camry.
Henry ran the place with his sons at first,
hardly comes in anymore—"Wife is poor,"
says Mark. I check out the cards
on the bulletin board: *Sally's Repairs*
and Alterations, Riding Lessons, a faded
photocopy, enlarged: *Life is a grindstone:*
whether it grinds you down or polishes you up
depends on what you're made of.

"How are you, Jan?"
"Good, living the dream, got new wheels."
"How's Joe doing?" "Thanks for asking.
His surgery's this month, can't do much."

A year ago, Henry and his sons sent me a card
when my wife died. She liked them—would talk
car repair with her. She'd have liked their Christmas
lights in March, framing the front door;
probably would have watered those geraniums
for them while she waited.

WHOSE WOODS

for Louie, October 2022

He was slumped over in his wheelchair when I arrived,
belted in, reading a large book nestled in his left arm,
his fisted hand holding the corner.

Looking up, he frowned, then smiled when I unmasked,
and greeted me with words I could not hear. Sitting close,
I told him of my day, then shared two poems,
and he came alive, pointing to the bedside table,
his hand trembling, where I found a worn Frost,
and read aloud, "I'm going out to clear the pasture spring,"
always a good place to start.

I passed the book to him, and he reclaimed his
reading glasses, turned the pages slowly, until he stopped,
looked up, his snow-whiskered face shaking, nodding,
and read, attending to each word, each phrase,
and I could hear nothing but the rhythms of his breath,
the sweep of easy wind and downy flake, until the end,
and he looked up again with the joy and wonder
that belie sleep.

WHAT WANTS DOING

"Otherwise, it's straight as a stick."
    Elaine, at ninety-nine

This morning, when I was making coffee,
you came from the bedroom in curlers
letting me know I was "okay, family"
and that you were good, too, today,
not that you would pronounce on anything.

It's just something you do, want to do,
have done since you were twelve
on your grandmother's Minnesota farm—
then, you say, you used rags to roll your hair,
and now it's plastic and Velcro.

You're right, doing what wants doing,
not that I would say anything either,
but they go with your smile, this good morning,
and unrolled, hair brushed, could inspire
an hour out for lunch, or most anything.

Elaine Curry, 2019, sepia ink and watercolor

GENERATIONS

Today she combs and braids her daughter's hair
before the windy beach, the sand, the sun,
gathering strands with practiced touch and care

each twist repeated in this moment's fun—
like one who long ago took her in hand,
three strands gathered, joined as one.

Her daughter dreams of running on the sand
with dancing feet and skipping braids
and waves frolicking, splashing on the land.

Tonight, she will undo the tired braids—
watching her daughter's hair fall casually
with grains of salty sand in a cascade—

giving thanks for daughters and the sea
for supple braids that hold and then come free.

Braids, sepia ink and watercolor

~ **3** ~

Shoes, ink and watercolor wash

THERE WAS AN OLD WOMAN WHO LIVED IN A SHOE

I'm sure she had her reasons.
Poverty—all those children—does sad things,
or maybe she lived green, ahead of her time.

You do wonder about the shoe though.
Maybe castoff work boots would have worked,
like those van Gogh painted:
the high tops, durable leather, sturdy soles.

I live in my shoes, just the one pair.
Size 10, fits the left foot fine but is too big
for my right. Enough space for a guest bedroom.
I built an addition, too, upgraded the ground floor
two inches in back, stepped it down to an inch in front.
The elevation improves the view, offsets my short leg.
I'm still a bit of a leaning tower.

A good house protects me from the rain and snow,
the scorch of summer asphalt, abrasive concrete,
the stub-your-toe edges of city life, even
out there somewhere, mother's mythic rusty nail—

but I remove it in the entryway,
less weight, more comfortable.
If I lived in the country,
I might just go barefoot like Huck
or all those children in the shoe,
making their way as best they can.

THE CANE

I did not want to use a crook-topped cane.
A walking stick, chopped from my back yard,
was better, rough and manly, tall and hard,
fit for climbing mountains, straightening pain.
And yet, increasingly on evening walks
I took the cane in hand, and with my wife
tread lightly on my pride for coupled life,
curved companionship, and simple talk.

I seldom think about my cane today
unless it hides behind a chair or door,
or throws a tantrum falling to the floor,
or runs away in a child's hand to play.
It's me and not me, this bent shepherd's staff,
chipped, worn, stable, strong, not my autograph.

DOPPELGANGER

I first saw him years ago in a store window,
a young man moving briskly but strangely,
his shoulders and head swinging in an arc
like a rocking horse, his body swaying
side to side like a small sailboat
tethered in light air.

I seldom see him; mostly I forget he even exists.
Sometimes before Christmas at the local mall
he jumps from window to window, Victoria's Secret,
The Gap, Williams and Sonoma,
swinging a shopping bag, then vanishing.

But he was here today in the polished glass wall
outside the clinic, still bobbing and rolling,
with a built-up shoe and jeans crumpled
at his right ankle, still moving along though
a bit slower and with a cane. He looked startled
when he saw me as if wondering who this man is
who walks with the funny gait.

ANXIETY

> *lean into the emotion—explore, write, write. let it drive the words.*
> A writer's prompt, notes

that might work if it were affection, like an earth mother holding her baby, or something like joy, square dancing and ready for a new partner, or ecstasy, a kite tugging on your heart string, or surely courage, that blazing sugar maple facing winter snow. there are lots of decent feelings you could lean into—happiness, love, grace, wonder, sorrow, even grief. they'd take your hand, lend a shoulder, caress you, maybe even cry with you.

but anxiety? give me a break. it's the fly in the kitchen, unpredictable, unwanted, unrestrained, unswattable. lean there and you're on the floor, face down, like a missed curb or your cane slipping on a wet tile, catching your breath, checking for broken bones, telling yourself you're all right, unconvinced.

as for driving, certainly—when you take the wrong turn, and you somehow end up in Revere at night, and it hits you, lost, and you're alone with the chain link fence and all the streets go the wrong way or say dead end, that's close; or the sound of metal scraping on concrete, fingernails on blackboards only worse, that crash you feel coming, the front of your car twisted, deranged, crinkled with worry lines, the tire, hanging loose, cockeyed, no way to ever roll again; or more likely, rear-ended, out of nowhere, by an idiot texting nothing, whipping your neck, your wind knocked out of you, gasping for air

on the floor again, sure as skidding on black ice or the taste of milk starting to go bad.

GOOD FRIDAY

The painters stripped siding off the back of the house,
refitted plywood sheathing, replaced flashing, then nailed
fresh clapboards, snug from the foundation to the gable.
Monday, they'll prime and paint, making it like . . . no,

better than new, which doesn't really work for this body
at this moment: maybe *dried out, cracked,* but *better*?
No way. Standing up is enough, like spring does—
a daffodil here, a crocus there. I'd be dead not to notice
the yellow bonnets and waist-coated robins.

                    When the painters finally finish,
a *hallelujah* no one sings will be in order; then they'll move
to the neighbors, scraping, replacing boards here and there, painting.

      Better to write it straight: *the world is flat today—*
no soil for roots, no sky for branching limbs—
then go to the store, buy *Cheerios* and the milk I need,
and for Easter something special. Try to be thankful—
tomorrow may be better—then walk the dog.

MY ROLLATOR

looks like the Eiffel Tower on wheels, sort of,
the struts curving down to four points for stability,
a folding seat for resting, midway, like the restaurant
platforms, and the spires stretching to the observation decks
where I brace my elbows and look out over the city,
except for the brake handles in front, looping forward and up,
like steer horns, and the chair handles jutting back
like the fins of a 1959 Cadillac. I'm tempted to add
a hood ornament, maybe Picasso's bicycle seat
with handlebars.

Towerwalker helps me tour from place to place,
except when I tilt, reach for my dog, fall and
gash my head, spilling a pool of blood on the sidewalk.
And you wouldn't know, but it's a wall whacker:
strikes door frames with thudding trusses;
carves gashes in paint; whips dressers, chairs,
what-have-yous with its brake wires; creaks under strain,
and bullfrogs complaints when you drag its vibrating wheels
sideways on a wooden floor. Outside, when I clomp along
the sidewalk, it's not "get your ticket at the station
on the Rock Island Line," not even Mississippi, Mississippi,
just Vermont, Vermont, Vermont.

APPENDECTOMY

It's so good to get my body back, like climbing
into the old Camry, knowing I will get there and back.

Hard when it's in for repair. They don't give you a loaner—
wouldn't handle right in any case, so you must make do,
laze about, play solitaire on the cell phone,
veg on the Red Sox, okay stuff but not the real thing,
any more than you can roll without wheels.

Not to romanticize bodies, we all know they can be a pain
in the kidneys, and they need regular servicing, washing,
and they finally wear out.

But when you get yours back, it's so good, like I said,
you just want to get in and drive away.

HOW TO SELF-ISOLATE

> *stay at home, in a room with a window you can open*
> Health Service, Ireland (https://www2.hse.ie)

For now, this window, bench, and tree will do,
will have to do: the bench, three stories down
across the street, sitting on the corner, not much
of a bench—more an overbuilt coffee table.

There are better benches with curved arms
and backs along the sidewalk to the north:
two seat toward the pond, another west
across Clew Bay to Croagh Patrick,
where I once sat and drew the holy mountain
early one morning,

                      and to the east,
one fronting Quay Street, the warehouses,
repurposed to shops, cafes, apartments; two others
attending the park and little pond, one with a memorial:

Greg Walker, Scottish Angler
Who fished these waters for forty years
"Great Fishing with Great People."

Few stop at the corner bench: that older man,
his road bike with panniers, all in black
tight clothes, who sat and checked his phone—
how far had he traveled?

                      The young woman
in a cotton dress with long dark-brown hair
that she twisted with her finger, then flicked
over her shoulder, stood, faced the bench,
and stretched like a runner, placing one foot,
then the other on the bench, leaning, dipping
. . . and walked off.

Behind the bench, some twenty feet,
the modest tree, a child catcher,

perfect for little ones who climb there,
the knobby roots like a stepstool,
thin low branches, fit for small hands;

    and the trunk, leaning, curving
the whole tree, bowing to the east, away
from Atlantic winds, like a saint with a hand,
palm open, fingers branching upward,
with leaves shielding the wind, the light rain
that fell yesterday, and the boy sheltering there,
almost invisible, until two other boys
appeared with a ball, and he jumped down,
and they ran off, passing it back and forth
on the wet grass.

    Westport, County Mayo, June 2022

The Child Catcher, pen and ink

CONFESSION

The impulsive enjoyment of life, which leads away both from work in a calling and from religion, was as such the enemy of rational asceticism, whether in the form of seigneurial sports, or the enjoyment of the dance-hall or the public house of the common man.
          Max Weber, *The Protestant Ethic and the Spirit of Capitalism*, 1904-5

I prob'bly shouldn't tell you this—
it's really nothing actually—
like when you retire, you wake up,
make coffee, and crawl back into bed,
mug in hand, and read poetry
or a schlocky novel . . .
maybe even sleep!

But last night I ate cake and ice cream
for dinner, not dessert. I was too tired
to cook, even to order out, and nothing
sounded good but chicken souvlaki and lemon
potatoes and the Greek place was closed.
My wife suggested it—the Haagen-Dazs
and left-over flourless fudge cake—
something I'd never done before,
and she was right, as usual.
Calvin's my side of the family,
not hers,

       and the paintings didn't fall
off the wall, and this poem waited,
unfinished, and my dreams weren't worse
than usual, and I'll stop for stop signs
when I drive, today, though, I admit,

I gobbled fresh strawberries, bananas,
walnuts, and blueberries for breakfast
—no shredded wheat, no skim milk—
and it was really good.

~ 4 ~

Sunflowers, ink with watercolor

ON LOOKING AT MY PAINTING OF SUNFLOWERS

> *Gaugin was telling me the other day that he had seen a very fine picture by Claude Monet of sunflowers in a large Japanese vase but— he prefers mine. I don't share his opinion—but I do believe that I'm improving.*
> Vincent Van Gogh, 1888

Van Gogh, of course, his were better. Does it matter? He painted sunflowers to decorate his studio in the yellow house when Gaugin came. Van Gogh gave him a fine canvas, too—their twisting heads, dashed in raucous chrome yellow, scruffy.

Ours were a gift from dinner guests. And the pitcher was a present, too, from a dear friend. All flowers are gifts, most hand-built pitchers, sometimes paintings. I try.

Do we really need another painting of flowers? Of sunflowers? It's sort of cheating, though the good kind. And it makes me feel good, which isn't nothing.

Sometimes it's hard to get inside a painting when it's flat. You can always reply on shape, line, color, rhythm, all that good aesthetic stuff, like the Modernists wanted. But this one's easy, maybe too easy—there's plenty of room inside to examine the light on the wall, the layered washes, or just roam around and remember.

There's my 4th grade teacher explaining heliotropism, pointing out the window at the sun. Me, too, planting sunflower seeds in the backyard that same year. Even Kansas, the Sunflower State and the Sunflower Hotel where my grandfather, Ralph, took me to a Lion's Club Luncheon and they served crunchy salmon patties. He was a towering man, a leader, as they said, with vision.

So come in, maybe just start with the flowers, with the one facing you, and the two in profile, one to the left, one to the right, even the back one looking away. Such symmetry, you could turn the pitcher and see the same thing four times.

How about the table, round like a sunflower, with those delicious shadows? That cotton tablecloth, those large checks that refuse to stay in line. Probably a kitchen table, a good place to sit and talk, though you'd have to move the flowers to one side to see each other. You can never go wrong with a kitchen table.

Have a seat with me, Van Gogh, my grandfather, and anyone else who wanders in. Ralph can tell you about playing football in Abilene against Ike in 1906. Maybe you have a sunflower story. Did you know sunflowers retire when they get old? They don't bother turning with the sun, like the science teacher said—just face east, hoping for one more good day.

ODE TO MY SKETCHBOOK

> *For he is good to think on, if a man would express himself neatly.*
> Christopher Smart, 1722 - 1771

For I will consider my sketchbook, Stillman.
For he feels good in my hand, substantial but not bulky.
For he is cat black, hardbound with signature binding.
For he boasts 124 ivory pages for contemplation and drawing.
For he is the progeny of N. Birn, Hamburg, NY.

For he likes to go bouncing on adventures in my daypack.
For he is patient, waiting his turn.
For he is hopeful despite evidence to the contrary.
For he listens, quietly, when I talk to myself:
    "I like this drawing, the curtain feels soft."
For he is a keeper of secrets, discrete in his silence.
"For he is a mixture of gravity and waggery."

For he is a connoisseur of ordinary things gathered in his folds.
For he displays a coffee mug, an old typewriter, a pot of basil,
    a window box.
For "Document" is his middle name.
For he serves as a coaster for that mug of coffee, temporarily.
For he is a still life that can do more than one thing at once.
For he conjures with sequence, creating an illusion of order.
For he is Buddha—just now, this page.
For he knows only God can spell, which isn't important.

For he is of the tribe of Codex, a venerable lineage,
For he still loves beauty, however rare.
For he is durable, a trouper, not likely to die or give up.
For he tolerates cross-outs, smudges, erasures,
For he puts up with watercolors, wrinkling with style.
For he enjoys the Spanish and French he doesn't understand.
For he memorizes inscribed quotations to be sure and true.

For he loves porches, even just lying alone on a table.
"For in his morning orisons, he loves the sun and the sun
    loves him."

For he holds onto things, faithfully.
For he helps me let go of things, put them down.
For he relishes "wicker," "daybed," and "porch," like any good poet.
For he leans on me when I doze, like Kit Smart's cat.
For he is a porch, part inside, part outside.

BLOOM!

Watercolor, wet-into-wet, is risky,
like a simile or driving into Boston.

Still there is joy in going there—
watching hues do-si-do on paper
like sour cream in cold borscht,
or dampening an edge to soften contrast
like mauve dusk blurring day and night—

until the point of a loaded brush touches
a too-wet wash and pigment gushes out
like ripples on a pond with rising trout
or a dandelion burst in a Fourth-of-July sky,
or better yet, like kids playing spud
on a grass-green lawn, running crazily outward,
screaming as the ball rises and falls,
until "it" yells *freeze,*

leaving a ruffled ring on your sheet
like a red zinnia on a snow-covered lawn.

WORKS ON PAPER

They say watercolors are passé.

Barefoot boys
no longer walk the Gloucester shore,
women climb mountains
but not in long dresses with parasols.

Manhattan skyscrapers refuse
to dance in the morning mist,
Maine lighthouses come pre-wrapped
in calendar art and postcards.

Not to mention watercolors are
small, ephemeral, and decorative:
no hard edge, no in-your-face color,
no impasto attitude or wall-sized ego.

Just landscapes washed across white paper
quiet as summer in the shade,
plazas sketched while traveling
shimmering in the summer sun.

People baptized with the touch of a brush,
splashing shadows across tables and chairs—
life laid down on paper
with deckle edges and a water mark,

fugitive and beautiful.

LANDSCAPE WORKSHOP

"If you're going to paint, just paint."
K. J., New Hampshire, 2022

This field, once a pasture, yellowed by the summer sun,
walled by grey-green trees soon to turn with cold nights

this field, now a place for Adirondack chairs, a bench,
for blueberries, rows behind me and to my right

this field with that island of stones and granite ledge,
topped by scrub trees, a small pine, upstarts.

"Simplify," she said, "you don't need individual leaves,
not even branches, the lines of your pen, just shape, color."

So I leave out the blueberries, the blue sky, the soil
and my patch of shade, the farmer who once worked here,

the pain in my hands, the worry, the thoughts of you
and your dying mother, yesterday and tomorrow,

and paint this field, once a pasture,
yellowed by the summer sun.

DOROTHEA LANGE: A GALLERY

IMPERIAL VALLEY, CALIFORNIA

On this grey day
flat as the horizon,
it is the migrant home
that takes you in

not the handsome father,
holding his swaddled baby,
or his old coupe, or the wash tub,
or the picking basket, even the boots,

soles up on the bench, suggesting
a body being eaten by the earth
like a Bosch painting. No, it is
the hut: its front like a crazy quilt

stitched together from pieces of
cardboard, fruit boxes, wood crates,
fragments of tar paper . . . so small
only stoop labor could enter,

with that little girl, hugging
the door frame, who
you finally see in
the black opening.

HIGH PLAINS

> *And I've got to be driftin' along*
> Woody Guthrie, "So Long, It's Been Good
> to Know, Yuh"

tall she towers
like the cumulus cloud
sweeping skyward
behind her

her hands
right on her forehead
left on her neck
say *hotter than hell*

her arms
italic thin
make a "W"
for worn

like her dress,
threadbare, a hole,
frayed, yet clean
and a smile

COMPOSED

> *California, Arizona, I make all your crops*
> Woody Guthrie, "Pastures of Plenty"

The solid, black Chevy
frames the father,
sitting on the back bumper,

clean shaven, clean dungarees,
glasses in his right hand,
he's good looking, patient,
waits for the click,
the crop, the oranges
what else can you do?

his little boy, three,
stands, enfolded
between his thighs,
clean, too, in his Sunday
best romper . . . *where's mom?*

and that hand, strong,
a working hand, cupped,
strokes his son's head,
comforts, touch as soft
as little-boy hair, hair he
parts slightly, revealing
that tilted dubious face.

SOUP KITCHEN

> *They used to tell me I was building a dream*
>   E.Y. Harburg, "Brother Can You Spare Me a Dime," 1932

workers caps
smart fedoras
with silk bands

jackets and suits
gather together
wait   stand   wait

one old hat shabby
banded with sweat
crushed   bowed

turns away
leans on the fence
hands folded

the tin cup cradled
on the rail.   empty
Give us this day

SISTERS

I would like to go to Boston to visit the museum.
I could rest under the shade oaks on the Fenway
just as well as in this churchyard.

It seems right to go now. We gave the painting,
my sisters and I, after the First War—
one hundred years ago,

and today is a perfect August day.
I would like to walk the halls to see where it is hung,
and mother's portrait, too,

to view that foyer, such dramatic light and dark,
the two vases, our adopted Japanese sisters,
and Florence, bless her, leaning against one,

indifferent, lost in shadow, and Jane at her side,
watching young Sargent (he loved his sisters, too).
Dear Mary Louisa, to the left, reticent, attentive,

all of us in our pinafores, not dressed, just there,
together, apart, and little me, with my doll
between my legs, pigeon toed, a bit precious, I admit,

but I was.

LIKENESS

Of course, my lips are fresh.
The tongue of your brush
kissed them with rose and crimson,
caressing Cupid's bow.

You compose my portrait for the viewer's gaze,
I sit at my mirror, composing myself for yours.
I gaze inward where you cannot see.

Silly man, with all your symbols,
that apple on my vanity,
as if you ever needed any tempting.

And marigolds everywhere, what do they mean?
Blooms of gold encircle my neck, faithful as the sun.
The wallpaper, a garden of Mary's gold,
but I am no more Virgin than Eve.
That solitary blossom in my hand:
Do I cast my fortune: He loves me, he loves me not,
he loves me, he loves me not?

At least you nestle a rose
in the halo of my golden hair.
I arrange each tress perfectly for you.
Only two strands remain undone,
trailing like tears rolling down my cheeks,
from eyes overflowing with longing.

Dearest, you paint too well for your own good,
capturing a likeness you do not see.

SEARCHING FOR FITZ

                      Though overcast
I drive to Gloucester to see if we can talk.
I've loved your work for fifty years:
well-crafted, shipshape, honest,
as optimistic as your time.

                                I stop
at Duncan's Point to see if you are in:
no luck, at least as far as I can tell.
Your studio, three floors up, is dark.

I walk around your granite home,
imagining the view atop your rocky
knoll: warehouse roofs, the inner harbor,
the jutting neck, Ten Pound Island, the sea
and that expansive sky you loved to paint,

when the clouds break,
spilling sun on water, town, and me—
not your luminous early morning light,
so warm, so soft, still, that blesses sails
and men in purest presence—

            but light, welcome light.

            ~

I stop by the museum on Pleasant Street,
Captain Davis's old house, now yours,
at least of sorts . . . "Gloucester's Own,"
they call you, local boy made good.

Your galleries are awash with tourists,
disembarked from a bus docked out front,
who peer at ships battling storms,
schooners safely anchored, all framed in gold,
some nodding, drifting from room to room,
others inspecting wall plaques, canvas sails, lines,
the intricate rigging of this maritime world,

while I stand and look at Riverdale, your pastoral,
so different and yet the same, the foreground boulders,
the wagon decked with hay, its wheels waking
the pasture with two tracks, the flat marsh
like a still cove, edged by trees with leafy sails,
and beyond, the old village with church steeple,
heaven-topped in the clouds of a high July sky,

even your signature single touch of red
on the shawl of a young woman, barely visible
walking along the stone wall, who catches my eye—
perhaps a Babson daughter walking home.
Twenty again, I walk with her, chatting,
to the edge of the canvas.

~

Your beach paintings were often spare,
a boat, rocks, the sky. On Pavilion,
you added a bit more—the island low
in the water, a distant brig dropping sail,
a schooner, foresail down, the waves beating
to shore, a small, beached yawl, one man
sitting on the gunnel, the other, red shirted,
pushing a wheelbarrow, and like always,
rocks and pebbles underfoot, tightly painted,
well defined,

                but still an everyday day,
like today: the island, the wind onshore,
with one determined walker, three folks
stooping, squatting, among the pebbles,
looking for treasures; and one young man
at water's edge—his black setter bounding,
running up and down the sand like a small boat
tacking in good air—who nods
and speaks as he turns to leave
holding at arm's length, pinched between
his thumb and index finger, a dangling
syringe and needle:

"Would be bad to step on this."

~

You composed
your Gloucester panorama from Rocky Neck:
obliging foreground folk admiring the scene,
lolling merchant brigs, tall masts, gathered sails,
anchored in deep water; small craft
making their way around the bay; the town,
wharves, waterfront warehouses, red brick
commercial buildings shoulder to shoulder,
and up the hill, white churches cresting
Middle Street, their steeples, silhouetted
against grey clouds, beacons of prosperity
and faith.

Making my way, I walk Middle Street
where you grew up, politely nodding
to merchant homes, dated and signed,
peering in yards, checking porches, windows
just in case you stopped by to visit
a friend or patron;

      then take the tree-lined gravel path
across the green to view the church:
its tapered steeple, towering skyward
with four tiers, like a ship at sea with sails set—
main, topsail, topgallant, royal—a ghost,
heading downwind on its final voyage.

~

This sunny, cold January day, I drive again to Gloucester,
to Eastern Point, where the cobalt-blue swells of the Atlantic
break white on dark rocks.   The August before you died,
you came here with friends and drew Brace's Rock
across the Cove to the South, the contour lines of your pencil

marking its bread-loaf shape, plus a sprinkling of salt rocks
exposed by the low tide, rippling lines for the caress of water
on the shore, and short, brisk marks to suggest foreground grass.

I've given up hope of talking to you (your paintings
do that in any case) but this seems like a good place
to try a final time. That winter, perhaps on day like today,
you painted in your studio a deserted cove and the rock,
starting with your sketch, adding an abandoned boat,
late afternoon summer clouds and light, and
the stillness of last years.

To get closer, I drive to the inner cove, making my way
on a small road, edged with large homes, and stop
near the signs that say

> *No Trespassing; Brace's Cove, Private Beach*
> *No Parking, Vehicles We Be Towed*

where I get out, and you say, "This way,"
nodding your head to a sloping sandy path,
lined with dry beach rose and dune grass,
and we make our way, you with your crutches,
me with my cane, till we spill out on the sandy shore,
and we stand there, side by side, alone, and just look—
the rock as it was and is and to the southwest
the low afternoon winter sunlight encircling
Gloucester clouds with a luminous halo.

Searching for Fitz, sepia ink and watercolor. This portrait is based on the only known photograph of the artist, *circa* 1860. The hand drawn map follows *The Map of the Towns of Gloucester and Rockport,* H.F. Walling, 1851.

LINES

are good for drawing hair.
It's all lines, not a simple contour line,
no cartoon balloon. Just lots of lines:

lovely lines, fine lines, ink lines,
sometimes short, sometimes long,
curved for twisting braids, sweeping for cascades,

overlaid strokes for texture, direction, body,
scribbles for thick dark turns, for shadows,
crazy squiggles for flyaways.

Lines are critical for poems.
Short or long, end-stopped
or not; rhythmic sound,

composed or found. And words,
of course, those unruly words,
the marks of written lines,

they bend, meander on their own,
shore lines, water lines, horizon lines,
and twist and snarl—worry lines,

distanced lines, testing lines, IV lines,
the hairline fractures
of an anxious world.

Still, you gather words, line them up,
stand them on end like dominoes,
carefully, until they're all in place;

then tip the first to watch it fall,
setting free the clicking rush to the last word,
the finish line.

~ 5 ~

Arlington Matins, ink and watercolor on Yupo paper

FLORIDA

is a green lizard, as I always say,
like that anole, climbing the screen,
looking for safety, sun, and mosquitos,
just like me—the safety and sun part,
not the mosquitos—I'm a strict vegetarian,
no insects, and I just flock here for the season,
a snowbird, Jersey goldfinch.

He's green as a lime, the leafing cypresses,
god, it's beautiful, this time of year, Easter,
that's how Florida got its name:
de Leon, that first invader, 1513, called it
Pascua Florida. Too bad Catholic
Conquistadors didn't worship lizards.

Speaking of Bishops, she called Florida
the "state with the prettiest name,"
one of her few laps of taste, but she was mainly
into mangroves, turtles, oysters, and birds—
the s-shaped ones, herons, egrets, pelicans—
nailed that part right. Doesn't even mention people.

Cannoli Anole, that's his name, is so cool,
got that great dewlap, with red-pink spots,
flashes it like an ascot under his chin for me,
turns me on something fierce, that and the way
he does pushups, nods his head,
moves as sly as a velvet do wop singer.
Together, we serenade street corners,
I do the back-up-line: "per-twee-twee-twee,
do wah, wah, wah," comes naturally, while he does
the falsetto, high as a swallow carving the sky.
Call ourselves, "The Flamingoes."

Cannoli's got lots of buddies here,
that's good, too, essential: they're what make
the sun shine. Makes Florida, Florida.
As they say, "With anoles away, it's a cloudy day."
Should be the state animal—the gator's

worthless, hardly eats any people.
You can almost see them on the flag—
two crossed lizards in blazing green,
a palm tree, and maybe a mockingbird,
singing in the silvery moonlight,
"I Only Have Eyes for You."

When Cannoli gets romantic,
he says we should move in together,
green and gold, a flashy ensemble,
and I'm tempted, we're both arboreal.
But it wouldn't work in the long run:
when it gets cold, he turns brown
(*anolis guacamolisis*), and flying lizards
turn into dragons, who eat birds. Me.

No, when I fly back home,
I will think of him, darting across the lawn,
sunning himself in his speedo by the pool,
singing *Kyrie eleison* Sunday morning,
and walking Honeymoon Beach with me,
my dearest, my "gota de cocodrilo,"
as Lorca would say.

HATS, A LOVE SONG

My hat it has three corners—
not really, none of them.
The Indiana Jones fedora comes closest:
in a pinch I could curl and tack
the brim to make it so

Three corners has my hat—
My English cap boasts eight tweed triangles.
I feel a bit of a Dickens when I wear,
like a newsboy in a 1930s movie, shouting
"Extra, Extra, winter is coming!"

And had it not three corners—
like my lazy-round cotton bucket hats,
blue, khaki, soft, saggy, that shade the sun,
say, "hi" to strangers, and doze in
my back pocket when I stop for coffee

It would not be my hat—
I refused to wear baseball caps for years:
too adolescent, jockish, until my love
bought me one at the shore on a cold
November day and I painted a watercolor

My hat it has three corners
and I wore it, three times three—
trimming it with shells and sand,
poems, talk, an afternoon walk,
until it fit perfectly.

THE GODDESS OF FUN

Her origin is unknown—surely not Mount Olympus,
nor the Garden of Eden, not even a suburb of Bethlehem.
Some say her mother was a fairy, her father, Santa Claus,
no immaculate conception, certainly. Others say
she simply is and always has been, giggling joy
like the sun's rays on a needful world.

She has no truck with vengeful gods on high
nor jealous devils below. She requires little—
no sacrificed lambs or sons, no penance,
crawling on knees, no fasting in a desert of guilt.
Not even the anguish of a godless world,
just silliness and play, daily laughter
and gathering weekly for coffee and strudel.

She takes many incarnations but I saw her
just yesterday on Main Street, her blue crocheted hat
aslant across her forehead, her red sweater
and sparkling necklace, puffy coat, fringed leather boots,
dancing through a pool of melted snow like a child
splashing in a puddle after a summer downpour.

THE TRUTH ABOUT SOURDOUGH

Was it the white upright stoneware crock,
that homey silo of domestic bliss
pictured in King Arthur's glossy catalog,
that made me order my "FRESH" starter?

Or was it simply February and cold
and I sat at our round kitchen table,
you away in Florida, and the thought
of sourdough brought back Berkeley,

1970s, where I bought crusty Toscana
at a local Lucky's, tearing it to share
with friends and lovers, while flakes
of crisp affection scattered everywhere?

I'm not sure, but I did, and my little jar
of starter arrived, promising to leaven my life,
maybe not *Lactobacillus sanfranciscensis*
of 49er stock but a proud Vermont pedigree

"lovingly nurtured for generations."
Little did I know that it would gobble more flour
for its feedings than I would use for the baguettes
and Jewish Rye of my heated imagination.

But—mixing sponge, flour, and salt,
kneading the shaggy dough into an elastic ball,
rise, re-rise, form, bake—I did manage to make
a crusty loaf, resembling a French beret

topped by a starfish, which I sit here eating
with butter—the crunch and a hint of sour—
imagining the artisan aroma drifts south
to waft you home to share a piece with me.

FRENCH FRIES

Downwind, fry oil from the cafe greets me in the parking lot.
I order at the counter between the postcards and beef jerky,
recalling drive-in fries served long ago with rubber-band clams.

Out back on the deck, the Gulf wind clears the scent
of memory and salts the air as I eat my fries, one at a time
until nothing but the stained paper basket remains
and fingers to lick.

I lounge on the rented beach chair underneath
a blue umbrella, sketching waves with fine ink lines,
thinking grey-green watercolors, while gulls, critics all,
kibitz overhead. I float on my back in the Gulf . . .

At grandpa's farm, dad drove the Chevy wagon packed
with cousins to the weedy lake with its mucky bottom.
It wasn't that great, but still I climbed the ladder
to the platform and jumped, holding my fear

with my breath until I hit the water with a slap.
Now I'll walk the shore until I come to a place
where the shells, broken but still lovely,
scatter their moon shapes like potato chips across the sand

and pick one up, almost whole, to take home.
No one will miss it.

RITUAL FOOD

Of course, Turkey: stuff with proper Dressing,
roast, slice, anoint with Gravy,
garnish with Gathering.

Christmas Eve we had Midwestern Oyster Stew.
I didn't eat but more than made do with Wedding
Cakes, cookie-cutter Santa Clauses,
and Aunt Jean's Spice Cookies, the recipe
she gave to mom, who made them
for my brother and me, and we made
for our sons, and they make for their kids.

But it's hard to take the Hot Dog seriously:
aka, frankfurter, wiener, or weenie, God help us.
I seldom eat for all the salt, fat, nitrates, and indigestion,
and yet on the Fourth, surrounded by family and flies,
I partake—the all-Beef kind, real American Meat
adulterated with ground baseball, fragments of flag,
and Sousa piccolos, God help us, properly burnt
on the grill, left over after all the chicken and burgers
are gone, and the chips, guacamole, and potato salad
are amply spilled on the paper tablecloth—finding room
somehow for sacred folly, puppy of Hot Summer Days,
topped with yellow mustard and eat in remembrance
of American Hope.

THRESHOLD

> *Passing through*
> *doorway after*
> *doorway after doorway.*
> Maggie Smith, "Threshold"

It's not just the sill, add the head and the jams:
that's better, but even more, an entryway or small porch helps,
even a good eave, a shaded overhang to lend betweenness,
a place to inhabit, to stand, to look out to the walkway,
or pause, upon return, before opening the door.

Or just think sunrise, twilight, or pussy willows, acorned lawns,
training wheels, wheeled walkers—you never forget how
once you learn—if that's easier, or smiling to strangers,
a nod and the sun comes out in a pleasantry of glances.

Some sanctuaries, especially simple ones with empty pews,
open windows, pregnant with still air, or just a commonplace,
a bench in a garden shaded by trees, where you can breathe.
Or a mountain top.

All rocky shores and beaches, for sure, and the cold water
that inches up your legs as you wade in until you launch,
close your eyes in the rush of water and emerge with a gasp.
Maybe an afternoon nap.

Halloween, of course, though only door-to-door
with a good moon to make shadows,
or a cemetery with carved slate headstones,
a door you can be on both sides of at once.

Most boxes with hinged lids, cave openings,
x-rays and ultrasounds, your body falling apart,
and certainly, sunken cheeks, paper skin,
holding hands and waiting.

Or maybe just putting words down, and more words,
until the lines shake and the page billows with smoke:
liftoff, sometimes, if you're lucky.

PADDLE

Such ease
    with a strong pull
        the kayak comes to life,
            another, another, it straightens, glides,
                points the way, moves with simple grace.

In open water
    I paddle bathed in sun,
        glowing inside and out
            sweating, my body warm,
            me, at one with me

    The water sings softly
        lapping on the bow, climbs aboard,
            dripping from my paddle
                with a cool touch and a smile.

In the stream
    the turtles line a log
        turn their heads slightly
            as I pass, give a knowing nod

    the lily pads flirt
        when the wind gusts,
            flapping the edges of their round skirts
                lined with red

    the pickerelweed whispers,
        the cattails salute
            when the blackbirds cry;
                a blue damsel fly, trim yoga lady,
                    balances for a moment on my arm

    the branches overhead
        share their shade, good neighbors all.
            I nestle down, stretching within the hull
                and close my eyes, still, still as still water,
                    just there, the world there, cradling me.

Returning home
    the wind at my back
        gives me a helpful shove,
            like the hand of a father
                pushing his son on a swing

INVOCATION

dear earth,
teach us to stand
like trees,

offering shade
like the oak
on a summer day,

pointing to the sky
like the spruce
to lift the spirit,

touching leaves to the ground
like the willow
to connect when lost,

making risky moves
like the birch
when too complacent,

celebrating change
like the sugar maple
turning crazy yellow-orange,

dancing en pointe
like the coconut palm
to tender a glimpse of grace.

SOME MORNINGS EVERYTHING IS A POEM

Bailey and I dog a bit in bed,
nuzzling and sniffing like lost friends.

Yesterday's white socks, one halfway in-
side out, hopscotch to the wicker basket.

The *Globe* on the porch delivers an opinion
piece on my wearing pajamas outdoors.

Without irony, the commuter train sings "Good
Morning, America" despite the disappearing blues.

In my palm, the gold jellybean of fish oil
conjures an Easter basket, complete with green

cellophane. As you catch an extra hour,
your sleep keeps quiet company over coffee.

Sunlight splashes iridescent in the sink,
inviting me to paint.

I have half a chapbook
by the time I brush my teeth.

ARLINGTON MATINS

The 87 bus trumpets, vroom—
God, I am so alive.

Across the street two trees chat,
wearing spring green

underneath, the hair salon and the cafe
hold hands in the shade

people float by, tethered to dogs and baby strollers
beckoning.

I sit on the front porch
feasting on granola and coffee

Berkeley, 1972, climbs in the window,
young and promising

music from inside joins me in the empty chair
Here comes the sun, do dee do do do

the day stretches out like Broadway
this day, and the ones to come.

This is the day that the Lord has made,
let us rejoice and be glad in it

God, I am so alive.

Acknowledgments

I wish to thank the editors of the following journals where these poems first appeared:

The Bicoastal Review: "The Imperial Valley," "Sisters"
The Connecticut River Review: "Appendectomy"
The Healing Muse: "The Cane," "The Meeting"
The Naugatuck Review: "How to Self-Isolate"
The Northern New England Review: 'In the Northeast Kingdom," "Landscape Workshop," and "Whose Woods"
The Tipton Poetry Journal: "Homemade"
The Unitarian Universalist World: "Invocation"

Some of the paintings and poems in this work were featured in a solo exhibition, *How to Write a Bench*, at the Anne Smith Gallery, Follen Unitarian-Universalist Church, Lexington, Massachusetts, October 29 to December 16, 2023. Thanks to Jane Spickett and Tempe Goodhue, curators.

I have been fortunate to receive encouragement and guidance from the community of poets during the last decade. As teachers, Jessie Brown, Steven Cramer, and Lee Desrosiers have been particularly helpful, serving both as muses and critical readers. Other poets have offered thoughtful reflection and the gift of friendship: Teresa Cader, Mariam Levine, Beth Kress, Hal Ober, Nancy Gera, James Carew, Nancy Brigham, Marge McMillan, Rachel Hyde, Carol Mitchell, Ruth Smullin, Kathy Leydon-Conway, Grace Solomonoff, and Susan Fry.

My growth as an artist has also been nourished by teachers: Kathleen Jacobs, Lucy MacGillis, Nancy McCarthy, Holly Bird, Rebecca Goodale, Stephanie Stigliano. Thanks to members of the Portrait Group of the Princeton Arts Society, with special hugs to Linda Johnson, David Lucht, Barbara Krashes, Bruce Dean, Ralph Caputo, Mary Pratt, Denis Coughlin, Tom Kellner, Debbie Kirk, Joanne Quinn, and Janice Raynor.

A Note on Ekphrastic Poems

Some of the poems in this collection are ekphrastic, speaking to specific pieces of art by other artists. Those who wish to view the inspiring artwork online should consult the following institutions:
"Searching for Fitz" (pgs. 62 - 66) addresses five paintings by Fitz Henry Lane at the Cape Anne Museum, Gloucester: *Gloucester Harbor at Sunrise, ca. 1851*; *The Babson Meadows at Riverdale, 1863*; *Ten Pound Island from Pavilion Beach*, 1850s; *Gloucester Harbor from Rocky Neck*, 1844; *Brace's Rock*, 1864.

"Dorothea Lange: A Gallery " (pgs. 56 - 59):
    "Imperial Valley, California, after "Mexican Field Worker's Home," 1937; Library of Congress.
    "High Plains," after "Woman of the High Plains, Texas Panhandle," 1938; Museum of Modern Art.
    "Composed," after "Porterville, Father and Son," 1936; Library of Congress.
    "Soup Kitchen," after "White Angel Bread Line, San Francisco," 1932; Princeton Art Museum.

"Sisters" (p. 60), after John Singer Sargent, *The Daughters of Edward Darley Boit*, 1882; Museum of Fine Arts, Boston.

"Likeness,"(p. 61), after Dante Gabriel Rossetti, *"Bocca Baciata,"* 1859; The Museum of Fine Arts, Boston.

Two of my poems also play with two well-known poems: "Talking to my Suitcase" (pgs. 11 - 12) with Frank O'Hara's "A True Account of Talking to the Sun at Fire Island;" "Ode to My Sketchbook" (p. 51 - 52) with Christopher Smart's "Jubilate Agno, Fragment B: 'For I will consider my Cat Jeoffry.'"

David Hummon is a poet, painter, and emeritus Professor (Holy Cross College, Sociology), educated at Columbia College and U.C., Berkeley. As an academic, he taught and published scholarly work on community, place identity, and related topics in American Studies. He also curated exhibitions at the Cantor Art Gallery, Holy Cross College *(Envisioning Jacob's Ladder: Religion, Representation and Allusion in American Visual Culture, 1750 - 2000)* and at the Worcester Art Museum *(Bostonians in Miniature: Portraits and Lives)*. Since retiring, he has focused his energy on poetry and visual art, exploring new ways to capture the character of people, places, and daily life through images and text. He currently lives in Winchester, Massachusetts.

Bench with Ivy, New Hampshire, aquatint print

www.ingramcontent.com/pod-product-compliance
Lightning Source LLC
Chambersburg PA
CBHW041805160426
43191CB00004B/65